Not a Lot, Robot!

by Marie Powell

illustrated by Amy Cartwright

A+
Smart Apple Media

Ideas for Parents and Teachers

These readers let children practice reading at early reading levels. Familiar words and concepts with close illustration-text matches support early readers.

Before Reading

- Discuss the cover illustration with the child. What does it tell him?
- Ask the child to predict what she will learn in the book.

Read the Book

- "Walk" through the book and look at the illustrations. Let the child ask questions.
- Point out the colored words. Ask the child what is the same about them (spelling, ending sound).
- Read the book to the child, or have the child read to you.

After Reading

- Use the word family list at the end of the book to review the text.
- Prompt the child to make connections. Ask: *What other words end with -ot?*

© 2015 Smart Apple Media, an imprint of
Black Rabbit Books
P.O. Box 3263, Mankato, MN 56002
www.blackrabbitbooks.com

Printed in the United States of America
Mankato, MN
2-2016
PA1322
10 9 8 7 6 5 4

Cataloging-in-Publication Data is available from the Library of Congress
ISBN: 978-162588-291-2

Illustrations by Amy Cartwright

Published by arrangement with Amicus.

Editor Jenna Gleisner
Designer Craig Hinton

This is my **robot**, Dot. She helps me with chores.

We have a lot to do today.
"Help me pick up my room,"
I tell Dot.

SPACE

SPACE

5

Dot picks up everything,
even my dog Spot.
"Wait," I say. "Not Spot!"

I tell Dot to make me a hot meal. Dot cooks pot after pot of hot soup.

"Not so much!" I tell my robot.

Next, I tell Dot to jot down spelling words.
But I don't want to study that many!
"Not a lot!" I say.

Then we take Spot for a trot. I am tired. But Dot keeps going.

"Dot!" I say. "Please stop."

At home, I lie on the cot.

"What's next?" asks Dot.

I say, "Not a lot, robot!"

Word Family: -ot

Word families are groups of words that rhyme and are spelled the same.

Here are the -ot words in this book:

cot	not
Dot	pot
hot	robot
jot	Spot
lot	trot

Can you spell any other words with -ot?